D1106444

TEXT MARCEL GINGRAS
PREFACE NAÏM KATTAN
TRANSLATED BY IAN FERRIER with MARIE-RENÉE COLLETTE
PHOTOGRAPHS
DR. MARTIAL MAROIS — MICHEL JULIEN

COLLECTION

SIGNATURES

Editor André Fortier

ÉDITIONS

P.O. Box 310 — LaPrairie, Qué.
J5R 3Y3 — (514) 659-4819

Éditions Marcel Broquet
Dépôt légal — Bibliothèque Nationale du Québec

ISBN 2-89000-050-8

PREFACE

In his painting, Henri Masson never departs from a theory, a well-defined conception of art. The landscape in his paintings has a story to it, a story that is not just a simple anecdote. Nature is modified, and to the colour the painter imparts. As he looks at the landscape, Masson is already re-inventing it. It becomes the product of his imagination, and this is how we perceive it. We look at it, and we order what we see according to a story we create for ourselves. Painting of this nature ends up corresponding to a landscape of our own imagining, with the stamp of our own spirit. Does the landscape truly exist if it is not revised and corrected by the painter? Of course it does, as long as we give ourselves the illusion that, in seeing what we see, we are all potential painters, but without the painter's added power to change the actual into a painting.

Masson's landscape does not just have a history. It is inhabited. With trees certainly, and with rooftops — while in the seascapes, small boats, lighthouses and fishing boats all show the presence of time. On the facades of the buildings, in the villages, towns, and hamlets, men inscribe their names into the passing moment. They are born and they die. They leave the boats and the facades of homes behind them.

Canada is a presence in his paintings, but as with all artists, it is his personal discovery. And he has fast asserted himself, alone, without the support of a movement, without the need to look for assurance from his emulators or his fellows in work and battle. Battle because it has been a real matter of combat: to assert himself as a painter, and to assert Canada as a landscape and a presence. It is after the event, once the painting is finished, that Masson can look at what he has done and say to himself he is a Canadian painter.

What captivates one most about a Masson landscape is that man is always present, even if he is not physically visible. The landscape is recaptured, worked, remade, before finally being reinvented by the artist.

When as an adult Masson returned to Belgium, the country of his birth — after all the years of preparing and working towards the realization of his purpose: to capture the world through art — when he saw the landscape of his infancy; when he rediscovered Europe, be it France, Italy, or above all Belgium, he was paying tribute to the fact that unconsciously, unintentionally, he was carrying a rich, weighty heritage. Without knowing it, he had continued with the attempts and the successes of the painters of his native country. One can say that Masson is an immigrant, in the sense that all Canadians are, in the sense that all artists are, though with a more pronounced accent. For he is an immigrant in the best sense of the word, in the sense where all men, and artists especially, rediscover their country each day as a new country. From this exile he excels, mastering the transitory in order to turn it into a permanent place.

Masson's vision is new. It is a twin vision, that of an artist, and that of an artist who has come from far away, with his memory and his heritage. He has carried to this new land the added dimension of that memory. He inscribes it into time, and makes of the moment an enduring history.

Henri Masson is an artist who sees, who knows how to see, who enables us to see.

Naïm Kattan

«At the end of the last century, in France, conventional art, I mean the art of Bouguereau, Gérome, Cabanel, etc... was official and all-powerful. It is now forgotten. In this, the end of the twentieth century, the people in power have changed their stripes, and recognize only what I call absurd art, the new at any price, the empty decorative, the abstract, pop art, op art, you name it! Nothing changes, except that this pseudo art is at death's door, if it is not dead already.»

These are the words of Henri Masson, a man whose canvases are sought after from Saint John's (Newfoundland) to Victoria, an artist who has succeeded not only without the *Establishment*, but in spite of it.

Strong-willed, straightforward and speaking without reservations, Henri Masson is a man who has always called a spade a spade. This disarming candour of his can be quite alarming if you do not know him, and even startles his acquaintances. Without doubt he has burned his bridges, notably with a few of the technocrats (let us not forget he has lived in Ottawa for 60 years) who cannot understand that a man of his talent did not fancy «*absurd art*» at a time when Canada was just discovering it, forty years after its prime.

Eclectic, cultivated, and open-minded, Masson can be the life of a party. He speaks of music like a connoisseur, and of politics like a man who knows what he is talking about. He speaks of his travels, but rarely of painting, preferring to leave that domain to action instead of words, to the work instead of to empty resolutions. Of course if the listener insists he will speak about painting, but only in terms comprehensible to the average mortal, in terms of the picture his painting portrays. With Masson everything is simple, clear, ordered. Painting is simply artistic expression, in the same category as sculpture or music: a spiritual necessity, a joy for its creator, and a pleasure for its recipient. Whether he speaks of his own painting or the works of others, we will never hear such terms as «a reaction that assaults us», «a search of self», «the expression of chaos», or «a step towards the absolute». If you tell him that artists are looking to create paintings of «significance», you will probably get a smile. Significant of what? Painting is painting to him. It is not there for soul-searching about values. It is an art. It is an art which he hopes has joys for both the practitioner and the beholder.

Today, having achieved both honour and renown, he still sticks to expressing himself with clarity, in conversation as well as in his art. He will not allow himself to succumb to the nonsensical jargon about painting that has been rampant in Canada for too many years.

One is still able to see this side of the man as one could in 1943, when in an article published in Le Devoir, Lucien Desbiens wrote: *«Masson does not paint to satisfy the needs of ailing intellectuals who, before anything else, look for a painting to be a literary work. Masson is much more simple. He has continued to use his unerring talent to translate the enchantments he finds in nature and the pleasures from everyday life.»*

Painting, sculpture, tapestry, music... all exist for

the pleasure of the human being. To apply political, sociological, or philosophical significance to art in general is, for Henri Masson, just as ridiculous and grotesque as making food into something other than it is. Food is for sustenance and for the pleasure it often gives us. We take art for what it is, a pleasure, an enrichment to the eye, the ear, the spirit, and that is that.

Of course some works do not turn out as well as others. Henri Masson is so aware of this that he has destroyed a number of his canvases. Furthermore, he has written into his will that all his remaining drawings should be screened by an already chosen expert with an eye to eliminating all that he deems unfit to survive.

Knowing his work, his admirers might find this quite severe, but anxious for perfection, the artist believes his public will be cheated if he offers them works with which he himself would not be satisfied. Henri Masson knows full well that a mediocre painting signed by a name artist will always find a buyer, but he is not interested in selling. If the inherent quality is not there, then it is not art.

The Obstacles

To follow such a calling and to make a living at it is not always easy. How could he help but know this, a man who for twenty-two years, from 1923 to 1945, had to be content to give only his leisure hours to what he loved, painting. So for twenty-two years he worked as an engraver in an Ottawa atelier, where he had at least the small consolation of being involved in an area affiliated with the arts. Furthermore, he produced works he could be proud of during this period, notably a chalice and paten the Oblate Fathers of Ottawa gave to the future Cardinal Villeneuve, on his appointment as bishop of Gravelbourg.

Since childhood though, he had been initiated into painting by the man he knew as his maternal grandfather, Arthur Bournonville, his grandmother's second husband. And having come to Canada in 1921 — with his mother, who dreamed of California, and whose marriage to a former Canadian serviceman, Albini Proulx, kept her in Ottawa — Henri Masson has always been drawing. As a young man, he got to know the painters of the Ottawa region. He worked with some of them, picking up technique from one, a sense of colour from another, but even then he interpreted these in a manner very much his own. Thus we never see him imitating or copying what he has found. Still young, he associated with renowned painters of the time, with painters who are famous even now — men such as Jean Dallaire, Franklin Brownell, Varley, Jack Nichols and a number of others. Later, he became a good friend of A.Y. Jackson.

All this time Henri Masson was an engraver, but he kept up with all that touched on art, music, and literature. He read widely, and he loved music. «*If there had not been music in my life,* he says, *I would have been a very poor man.*» For all these early years he was not just an engraver, but a man interested in the whole artistic domain.

The Caveau

As luck would have it, for him and for a number of other artists in Ottawa-Hull area, a remarkable institution called the Caveau was founded in 1933, by the Dominican Fathers of Ottawa. The inspiration for a renewal of the cultural order (just one example was their excellent Dominican Review), the Dominicans wanted to offer painters, musicians, thespians, and writers, a place to meet with each other, a place where each could profit from the experience of the others. Henri Masson was just 26 years old. At the Caveau he would meet Guy Beaulne, Father Georges-Henri Lévesque, Marius Barbeau, Jules Léger, Léopold Richer... and together, the habitues of the Caveau became an animating force in Ottawa cultural life, a force that laid the foundation for Ottawa cultural life today, at least in its French elements.

It was not until 1938 that he held his first important exhibit, at the *Picture Loan Society* in Toronto. It was a succès d'estime, not much more. He returned two years later, selling a drawing to A.Y. Jackson, and two canvases... to the proprietor, Douglas Duncan. Enthusiastic collector, amateur dealer, compiler of art works and patron to David Milne, Duncan assembled a significant art collection in his lifetime. It was inherited by his sister, Mrs. J.P. Barwick, who donated it to forty-four establishments of various types throughout the country. Of the collected works, 634 were offered to the National Gallery of Canada. They included one of two canvases bought from Henri Masson in 1940, unsigned and dated 1938.

In 1940 Masson exhibited forty canvases at the Caveau. He sold one, for fifteen dollars.

Patience

When he recalls these first sales, the artist smiles at the impatience of the new generation of younger artists. To the ones who aspire to glory the day after they first pick up a paintbrush or a palette knife, he advises patience, remembering that ten years of craft went into his first exhibit.

To any young artist avid for recognition, Henri Masson will say that a painter's fortunes depend on a number of different factors. He will speak of the disappointments of painters who only received recognition after their lifetimes. He will say that our painters do not always get the recognition they deserve, and that poverty and destitution have struck down more than one. He will remember Marc-Aurèle Fortin, Jean Dallaire, Paul-Émile Borduas, David Milne and Emily Carr, to name just a few well-known Canadian painters, each one of whom had to endure many a dark hour.

«*The time comes,* he says in closing, *when a painter finally finds some reward*». For Masson this time was 1942, and an exhibit in Ottawa where he sold every single piece. Three years later he could end his work as an engraver. He could devote himself wholly to his art and make not just a living at it, but a good one.

Poverty is not the life for him. He has always made a decent living, first in the engraving trade mentioned, and later through his art. He is a worker. Although comfortably well-off now, morning still finds him awake at seven o'clock. And his talents have served him well, finding him favour first with such patrons of the arts as Harry S. Southam, and later with what quickly became a national audience for his work. From east to west, throughout Canada and abroad, his paintings have progressively passed through the doors of all the important galleries, and for many years now the demand for his work has been so strong he cannot keep up with it. Despite this, he maintains his concern for the quality of his work, knowing full well that time will make allowances for the true creator where it tends to overlook the mediocre.

The Artist at Work

Orderly and methodical, Masson sets to work as soon as he wakes up. In the calm of his studio, to the sound of chamber music drawn from his record library, he will drink the coffee he has made and aim a critical eye at the painting he worked on the day before.

Henri Masson likes his studio. But for all he enjoys it, do not think for a moment that he will not paint anywhere else. Quite the contrary. It is in the picturesque streets of Canadian towns, in Quebec above all; it is in natural surroundings, be they open country or seashore; these are the places he likes to work. «*Art and nature go together. Beauty is not subjective*», he will say, citing Rodin. He will even paint sitting in his car, saying he has always been fascinated by umbrellas and by the way water reflects on the roadways.

At the beginning of the thirties, when he did not own an automobile, Henri Masson was limited to painting the streets of Ottawa and Hull, which he could reach by street car. Both these cities have since undergone huge transformations, and his canvases from that period are now historical documents. «*To tie the present to the past is a necessary act*», said Rodin. As early as 1950, *Time Magazine* has termed Masson a «*raconteur*».

In 1935, having bought his first car, he started his excursions through the Gatineau, the Lièvre valley, Ripon, and Montpellier. He has now been painting in the Gaspé for twenty years; for ten years he has worked in the Charlevoix region, the Eastern Township, and Ontario. In 1954, profiting from a stay at Banff, where he taught for a Summer, he made some paintings of the Rockies. He has been to Newfoundland twice. He has painted in France, in Italy, and in Portugal, but «*I am a Canadian*», he says. «*Canada, and especially Quebec, are the first places I paint.*»

His work contains paintings of musicians, the odd still-life, nudes hardly ever. There is not one portrait. Sure he will do a painting of two women playing music, or a couple of the neighbourhood children, but a portrait as such: never. He leaves it to others to immortalize the greats of this world.

He has touched on all forms of expression open to a painter — drawing, watercolours, pastel, ink, and washes — but oils are what he prefers. They compose ninety percent of his work.

Musiciens, study

The Road in Winter, 1970
Charcoal, 45,5 x 64,5 cm
University of Ottawa

Bourget Lake, 1978
Charcoal, 45,5 x 61 cm
Collection : Mrs. Jacqueline Brien

To start a work in oil, or just for the sheer pleasure of it, Masson will do drawing after drawing, often with colour or notes on colouring. Does he have any need to note them? «*After fifty years, you understand, once I look at a landscape for an hour or two, I know what I want from the subject*», says Masson. He adds that he has never worked from a photograph. «*A photograph, it is wrong from the point of view of painting, the perspective is wrong. But for all that, an artist should not be rebelling against the new. He should try everything, he must have an ongoing sense of experience.*»

Though Masson will indeed try anything, he is also the possessor of a distinctive style. His themes and his subjects are varied, but always recognizable as his. Nevertheless he objects to any trademark which might identify him with a particular theme, and points to the artists we recognize immediately by their choice of subject, often limited, and by the way all their paintings seem the same.

> «*Art is an adventure. At the beginning of a painting one never knows how it is going to end up. That is what creation is all about. Instinct plays a huge part in art. In all, painting demands a truly alert spirit, constantly wide awake, even when driving a car. To paint, one must always be on the lookout.*»

Teaching; Conferences

> «*I have never taught full-time*», says Henri Masson. «*Full-time teaching is death for a painter.*»

Though never full-time, he has still taught at a number of places: at Banff in the summer of 1954; at Queen's University, six weeks a summer for five years; at the Doon School of Arts for three summers, a few weeks a summer; at major scholarly institutions in Ottawa; and at the National Gallery, where he gave courses for children. Over the years he has also taught at his studio for a morning or an evening, but never more. When a New Brunswick university offered him the post of artist in residence for an entire year, he refused.

But conferences? Hundreds! Hundreds of what he calls «chats», or «talkfests». Certain that the listener does not retain much of what he hears, he is nevertheless happy to have attended. He gets a lot of pleasure from the human contact, and enjoys the chance to exchange viewpoints and listen to the opinions of others.

Music

The Masson who said he would have a pretty poor life without music is a man with a real mania for it. His record library amounts to some 2,000 records, and he listens to them religiously for two hours a day. Given another odd hour, he will fill it by comparing different recordings of the same piece. He is also the owner of a magnificent stereo system, his only «show off» possession, he says.

His musical tastes are «catholic», he adds, in the first sense of that word. He will listen to baroque or modern music with equal pleasure. Nevertheless he still has his preferences, and some composers he just cannot abide.

Near Rupert, Que., Oil, 45,5 x 61 cm
Collection: Mr. Gilles Fortin

The Violin, 1960, Oil
Collection: Mr. and Mrs. A. Larivière

He likes Bach, Vivaldi, Haydn, Mozart, Schubert, and Beethoven. He likes Berlioz a lot, along with Chausson, Ravel, Debussy and a number of others.

Of the twentieth century composers, he has been listening to Mahler for 25 years, since long before he became the fashion in Canada. He adores Sibelius, «*a very great musician who makes me think of my country, Canada*», he says. Among contemporary composers, he gives preferences to Shostakovitch. He owns the fifteen quartets, which he finds absolutely splendid. He also favours a few of Bartok's quartets, particularly the early ones.

Now that he is talking, Masson adds, «*I like this, I don't like that,*» and goes on to clarify: «*There are musicians I detest profoundly. For instance, Satie.*» Who else? «*I like Prokofiev a lot, and Benjamin Brittain; Penderecki is one of the foremost of the moderns. He has written a really moving cantata on Auschwitz. He wrote some quite astonishing music, and modern in the true sense of that word, but now he has returned to tonality and melody, to a music accessible to more people than just the purists. Obviously,* he continues *those opposed to harmony do not like it. It is like people who do not like communication in painting. This does not go down well with me. My tastes in music are like my tastes in painting. I read a lot about these musicians, and I like to be able to find them in their works.*»

Having enlarged on his taste in composers, Masson moves on to talk about different musical genres. We learn that he loves chamber music, and does not much like opera. He does enjoy a few works by Strauss: Salomé, Der Rosenkavalier, Electra; the latter especially, for its marriage of voice and orchestra. We learn too that he detests electronic music, and that he cannot stand anything by Stockhausen.

Using a word he is fond of, he says he has no patience with «musiquette,» or trivial music. «*I do not have time for it. It takes time to listen to Beethoven's 16 quartets. One has to listen, and I listen to them regularly. A man who has never thrilled to the sound of one of these last Beethoven quartets has really missed out.*»

Reading

A real music enthusiast, Henri Masson is equally a great reader. He has read a tremendous amount on the subject of musicians and painters, and possesses a fine library on art and on works of art.

His reading does not stop at these two subjects though. As a teenager, like everyone he had to read the classics in school, but he was bored by all but Molière. He was much happier reading Voltaire, Rousseau, Hugo, Zola, Balzac, Flaubert, Tolstoi, Dostoevsky, and the English classics. «*At 18, Hugo was my idol.*» *In Ottawa, where Louis Veuillot and Léon Bloy were required reading, I was laughed at.*»

Even if he did read Montherlant and other contemporary writers, and never Proust or Claudel,

Masson says he really prefers reading about history and social matters. He subscribes to a number of magazines, but does not find much time for them. His main preoccupation has been with the fortunes of his fellow men. He feels that the man who does not revolt against war, against injustice, and against the plight of the millions of the poor who die each year, is worthy of contempt.

Plants

Aside from music and painting, Henri Masson also enjoys cultivating plants. He had a greenhouse during the years he lived on Spruce Street in Ottawa. He knew every plant in it, and should the occasion have arisen, he could have predicted when each would bloom to within a day.

He does not have a greenhouse in his new home, but bathing in the light of its huge windows is a winter garden. There he has arranged many green plants alongside a small palm tree, a lemon tree, an orange tree: a miniature tropical forest. Why this winter garden? Because it is a bit of the natural world brought indoors. «*It is a way of expressing love for life*», says the painter.

As his wife looks on, he says:

> «*We have always loved plants. We have always bought paintings and records too, not to show them off, but for the joy they bring us. Lately we have been buying bronzes. When you own a work of art it is for the joy of it, not so you will get compliments. Art is an intimate thing, something you should live with, like plants. The man who has the gift of being able to enjoy these things is a wealthy man.*»

> «*We are preparing ourselves for the last part of our lives. When we can no longer travel we will still be in pleasurable surroundings. One must always look at the present, take some thought for the future, and forget the past. This life is a beautiful one.*»

Reflections such as these might surprise those who think of him as a cold man. He is an extremely warm person. One just has to listen to the affection in his voice as he talks of his wife's kindness, or her gentleness.

Painters

Painters are not generally known for the way they shower praise on their confreres. Is Masson any exception? Of Canadian painters, he really likes Emily Carr and Varley, and these are not the only ones.

> «*Of the painters of my generation*», he says, «*I have a lot of admiration for people like Surrey; Roberts is an authentic artist; Pellan, a pioneer in Canada; Borduas has his place too. As you know, I am not an abstract painter. I cannot go along with that obscure manner of seeing things, nor with decorative painting, but if I put myself in someone else's place, I can see it through his eyes.*»

The Studio in June, 1981, Oil, 96,5 x 114 cm
Masters Gallery, Calgary

The Studio on Bruce Street, 1969
Watercolour, 61 x 76 cm
Collection: The Artist

Anemones, Nice
Watercolour, 35,5 x 43 cm
Private Collection

Masson now switches to the subject of foreign painters, and says that Rembrandt is his favorite for drawing. He says when he visited the Prado in Madrid, Goya was a revelation for him. He states his admiration for Bonnard by saying he would prefer one of his paintings to a canvas by Picasso, however much he recognized the genius of the latter.

Throughout the discourse he devotes to the subject of painting, Masson often returns to the importance of drawing in the work of a painter, and he deplores the extent to which so many good artists of the twentieth century have been neglected.

An excellent draftsman himself, he respects those who know how to draw. His preferred choice is Rembrandt, but he is also partial to Dunoyer de Segonzac, and in fact owns one of his drawings.

Scarcely a Masson at Masson's House

Henri Masson is a collector, but only a collector of the works of others, not his own. You cannot find ten of his works at his house. On the other hand, if you look for the works of others you can find marvels: drawings, paintings, and sculptures.

Just by itself his collection of drawings is something to behold. Sketches by: Cullen, Dallaire, Sylvia Daoust, Derain, Dunoyer de Segonzac, Raoul Dufy, Clarence Gagnon, André Biéler, Henri Hébert, A.Y. Jackson, Osias Leduc, Arthur Lismer, Pascin, René Richard, Suzor-Côté, John Fox, and others.

In his hunt for the works of others, has he ever found masterpieces for a song, the ones we hear all the collectors talking about? Never! He says that of course he has found «bargains,» but only because all paintings turn out to be either that or close ot it. As such he once picked up a beautiful watercolour by Marc-Aurèle Fortin for $125. He has made exchanges too, notably one with Fortin at a time when the latter's paintings sold for $35. But never bargains, never the finds you hear about in the papers from time to time.

One might be a little taken aback at finding the abstracts in the artist's collection: a Bellefleur, a Shadbolt, two or three others at most. Masson explains: «*Temperamentally, I am not inclined to buy many non-figurative works. I am a man at the same time as I am a painter, and when I buy a painting it is the man who generally makes the choice. But as a painter, I will sometimes buy other things. All my impulses as a man want clarity, nature, man expressed in a poetic fashion. There are certain artistic manifestations my instincts refuse. It is all a question of temperament.*»

According to him, art must communicate. The viewer of a painting should feel what the painter feels, feel what he wants to say, without explanations. That is the important thing.

> «*What bothers me is people who have to explain a painting. When I go to a museum and listen to some of the incredible nonsense the guides spew out, I get a kick out of it. These guides have a vocabulary that is a joke, completely incomprehensible.*»

Talk to the artist about the «Objective Reality», or «Hypnagogic Images», etc., and he will howl.

To sum up, Masson says:

> *«I think non-figurative painting has a place in airports or railway stations, places you pass through quickly. That way you do not have to look at it for too long.»*

The Establishment

Just by themselves, the artist's thoughts on what he calls the *Establishment* would fill a volume. To summarize: he does not like the Art *Establishment* or its centre in Ottawa. Why? Because according to him they are not playing their role very well. By the *Establishment*, Henri Masson means the National Gallery, the Art Bank, and the Canada Council, to name just a few of its manifestations. He says, «*The whole area needs to be cleaned up. All its policies are in the hands of a few small men who play with too much power and end up managing everything. They manage because either out of ignorance, or out of fear of offending an influential colleague, the politicians would not interfere.* According to the artist, politicians should get up in Parliament and denounce these fools who trade in the millions of dollars which gets set aside for the purchase of «*trash*». «*Anonymous, powerful, and totally cynical,* says Masson, *the people of this Establishment know they can sleep in peace, protected as they are by politicians who, for their part, are afraid of being laughed at for denouncing these extravagant purchases, of being told they do not understand.*»

Masson himself does not need the *Establishment*. He has enough trouble trying to keep up with the galleries' demand for his work. So it is in thinking of the young, talented figurative painters that the artist speaks as he does. «*Considering the whole history of art,* he says, *the impressionists were overlooked for years.*»

To conclude this chapter in all objectivity, one has to mention that Masson has not always been treated poorly by «Official Art,» the other name he gives to the *Establishment*. Between 1943 and 1957, the National Gallery bought six of his works. In comparison, in about the same period it bought seven Cosgrove and six Borduas. We can add too, that of the six Massons, four have travelled widely since entering the Gallery's collection. For instance, a painting of children cleaning a skating rink was exhibited at the Morse Gallery in Florida in 1943, at Yale University in 1944, and at the University of Maine in 1951. Another, entitled «Skaters», was shown in Washington in 1950. A still life exhibited for the *Florida State Fair* in 1952 could be found two years later on display in New Delhi, India. As a final mention, in 1951 another Masson work, property of the National Gallery, and entitled «The Joy of Summer», figured among an exhibit of paintings at the Biennial in Sao Paulo, Brazil; Borduas' «Unforeseen Eruption,» to name just one other work, was also among the select company shown.

What rouses Masson's indignation the most about these lords of official art is not their ignorance as much as their tendency to only choose the offbeat, to the detriment of all young figurative painters. He notes, however, that among the art

Gaspe, 1978
Oil, 56 x 71 cm
Collection: Dr. and Mrs. M. Marois

Freshwater, Newfoundland, 1970
Oil, 30,5 x 40,5 cm
Private Collection

Autumn Scene, Oil, 40,5 x 51 cm
Collection : Mrs. Louise Marie Laberge

dealers and auctioneers, figurative work is still the most popular. If official art makes a mistake, the collectors do not.

Exhibits

Except for those of us who were not even eight or ten years old in 1972, most of the people in Canada have had the chance to see, if not a canvas, then at least a reproduction of a Masson painting. For in that year a Masson painting was one of the motifs chosen by the Canadian Postal Service for their Christmas stamps. And two years before, the whole world had the opportunity to see a reproduction of a Masson. UNICEF had chosen one of his canvases as the theme for a Christmas card.

It is hardly an exaggeration to say that the card and the stamp were Masson's two largest exhibits. His other exhibits, these in the more usual sense of the word, are numerous. The series started at the Caveau in 1933, 1934, and 1935, when the artist exhibited drawings, paintings and watercolours. In 1936, he exhibited his first oil painting, and Carl Schaefer sent him a letter containing high praise for the piece.

These were all group exhibits. It was not until 1938 that he put on his first solo show, at the previously mentioned *Picture Loan Society.* We will pass quickly to a time three years later, when at the same place, he sold his first paintings. In the interim, the *Canadian Group of Painters* had chosen him as an exhibitor in 1939, quite an honour considering his name figured alongside such renowned artists as Jack Humphrey, André Biéler, A.Y. Jackson, Louis Muhlstock, and others.

That same year, a Masson canvas appeared in the New York World Fair. More than thirtv years later, in 1970, another Masson canvas appeared in an international exhibit in Osaka, at the Quebec pavilion. Here it should be mentioned that he was the only non-Quebecois painter in the exhibit. Since he had painted so much of Quebec, they asked him for a canvas, and he sent them a scene he had painted of Chicoutimi-Nord.

But to get back on track we should return to 1940, when everything, we might say, got rolling. That year Masson exhibited in the 57th Spring Salon at the Galerie des Arts in Montreal, with sculptors Robert Pelletier and Sylvia Daoust, and painter Jean-Paul Lemieux. The painting he sent was entitled «Icehouse».

In 1942 he exhibited at the Addison Gallery in Andover, Massachusetts, this time in the company of A.Y. Jackson, Philip Surrey, Lawren Harris, Edwin Holgate, David Milne and Goodridge Roberts.

That same year saw him at l'Art français in Montreal, with an exhibit which would finally launch his work into every serious gallery in the country. A list of these can be found at the end of the text.

His name would be renowned from then on. His paintings would be seen in major international exhibits; the National Film Board, in 1944, would make a documentary immortalizing him with the likes of Marc-Aurèle Fortin, Jean-Paul Lemieux, Alfred Pellan and André Biéler. Radio and then television would harry him for interviews. One of his paintings would even appear on the cover of the Federal Government's phone directory in 1980....

The Collectors of Masson

Among Masson aficionados we find people of all ages. The ones who touch him the most are the young, working to buy a painting they like on the «installment plan». But his audience also extends to very wealthy organizations such as oil companies, who along with the galleries, are all involved in the hunt for his works.

The artist himself is not inclined to vanity, but perhaps he will allow us to mention that Princess Alice, the aunt of George VI and wife of the Earl of Athlone, a Governor General of Canada, bought one of his paintings in 1941; that in 1967, the Canadian Government's wedding gift to Princess Margriet of the Netherlands was a Masson; that the uranium magnate Joseph Hirshhorn has bought a number of Masson works, as have many of the Canadian Provincial museums, etc.... We can add too that a Masson was Canada's gift to mainland China in 1971.

A list of his important buyers must also contain the name of businessman Harry S. Southam, whose generosity was also responsible for the donation of a number of Masson's paintings to various Canadian museums.

Masson's work then, can be found on most of the continents of the world. But he is always particularly happy to see his paintings in Canada, and happiest to see them in the hands of modest collectors who, along with himself, ask that art embody a feeling for life and for the joy of living.

The Man

Henri Masson is a force of nature. That is what we feel on first meeting him: the strong handshake, the sonorous voice, the sparkling eyes, close to six feet of the man, and with the shoulders of an athlete.

This man, who has made the world of Canadian art proud, just missed not being a Canadian at all. He was born in Spy, a Belgian hamlet near Namur, on the 10th of January, 1907. He lost his father at the age of twelve, in 1919. Armand Masson, a glazier by trade, and a voracious reader and music lover, died at the age of 37, a victim of a cerebral embolism. The First World War was coming to a close, and like many Belgian families, the Massons had known hard times.

The artist's mother, born Berthe Solot, moved to Brussels after the death of her husband. Two years later, however, dreaming of the sun, she decided to leave Belgium for California. On the way to the new country, she stopped in Ottawa to look up the first Canadian soldier she had met in Belgium during the war. She never left. During her stay she met the Canadian she married, Albini Proulx, who would be her companion for the next thirty years.

That is how Henri Masson became a Canadian. He returned again to Spy for the first time in 1952, and it was quite a party: a civic reception;

Choir-boys, Study
Pastel, 30,5 x 23 cm

Monks Reading, Oil, 56 x 66 cm
Collection: Mr. Carl Masson

conversations with Arthur Chavée, the burgermaster; looking up childhood friends, and more...

Henri Masson thus passed his adolescence in Ottawa, and interspersed with many trips through North America, Europe, and Asia, he has remained in Ottawa his whole life.

In 1929 he married a charming woman, Germaine Saint-Denis. The Massons had three children: a daughter, Armande, who has realized the dream of her paternal grandmother by going to live her life in California; and two sons, Carl and Jacques, both of whom live in Montreal. Mr. and Mrs. Masson now have ten grandchildren and two great-grandchildren.

Over the years, the Massons lived close to the Dominican Monastery in Ottawa, a proximity which has brought to art lovers all the marvellous paintings Masson has done of monks and choirboys.

They have now moved to a newer part of Ottawa, and live in idyllic surroundings: a house bathed in sunlight, filled with green plants, and furnished with exquisite taste. The decorations are paintings and bronze sculptures, mostly figurative, and he has chosen them with love from among the works of artists he truly enjoys.

Not lovers of television, Mr. and Mrs. Masson prefer music and reading to all other pastimes. They still enjoy entertaining and going out to see friends, and are both especially happy when their children and grandchildren can get over for a visit.

If the painter spoke earlier of old age, it does not seem imminent now. He remains active, in his studio and in the great outdoors, and his high-spirited discussions on social questions give one the impression that old age for him is as George Sand described it:

«*It is wrong to believe that old age is a downhill slide; it is the opposite. We climb, and with surprisingly large steps. Intellectual work now comes as easily as physical work to a child. One still approaches the end of one's life, not as a peril, but as a goal.*»

Marcel Gingras

Carl Sleeping, 1941, Charcoal, 45,5 x 63,5 cm
Collection: The Artist

Country Dance, 1940, Oil, 35,5 x 40,5 cm
Collection: Mr. and Mrs. Jacques Lalonde

The Spectators, 1941, Watercolour, 38 x 53 cm
L'Art français, Montreal

Perkins, Que., 1950, Charcoal
University of Ottawa

Winter Landscape
Charcoal, 45,5 x 63,5 cm
Private Collection

Winter Landscape
Charcoal, 45,5 x 63,5 cm
University of Ottawa

Under the Bridge, Old Chelsea, Que., Watercolour, 35,5 x 45,5 cm
Private Collection

Old Chelsea, Summer 1947, Watercolour, 51 x 30,5 cm
Private Collection

Nicky
Charcoal, 40,5 x 30,5 cm
Private Collection

The Two Brothers, 1973
Charcoal, 38 x 25,5 cm
Private Collection

Carl and Jacques, 1944
Ink and Pastel, 35,5 x 43,5 cm
Collection : The Artist

Alcove, Que., 1950
Oil, 38 x 45,5 cm
Private Collection

Forest Interior, 1955
Watercolour, 38 x 45,5 cm
Private Collection

Rocks and Snow, 1948, Oil, 56 x 76 cm
Musée du Québec

The Chignon, 1961, Casein, 45,5 x 38 cm
Galerie Vincent, Hull

The Three Monks, 1950, Oil, 38 x 45 cm
Musée du Québec

St. Irenee, Charlevoix Cty., Oil, 30,5 x 40,5 cm
Collection: Mr. Gilles Fortin

Fishermen at Gaspe, 1950, Oil, 45,5 x 56 cm
Private Collection

Summer Landscape at Wakefield, Oil, 56 x 66,5 cm
Musée du Québec

Summer Landscape, Oil, 45,5 x 56 cm
Private Collection

Double Portrait of Philippe, 1979, Watercolour, 38 x 46 cm
Collection : Dr. and Mrs. M. Marois

The Offering, 1969, Oil, 30,5 x 40,5 cm
Collection: Mr. Claude Laberge

First Snow, Booth Street, Ottawa, 1980, Oil, 40,5 x 51 cm
Private Collection

Skaters at Hull, 1974, Oil, 40,5 x 51 cm
Private Collection

Skaters, Oil, 30,5 x 40,5 cm
L'Art français, Montreal

Back from School, Oil, 25,5 x 30,5 cm
L'Art français, Montreal

Gaspe Landscape, 1979, Oil, 61 x 76 cm
Collection : The Artist

Grande Vallee, 1980, Oil, 56 x 71 cm
Downstairs Gallery, Edmonton

Indian Harbour, Nova-Scotia, 1966, Oil, 30,5 x 40,5 cm
Private Collection

Riviere au Renard, Gaspe, Oil, 61 x 81 cm
Private Collection

Landscape near Buckingham, Que., Oil, 45,5 x 56 cm
Private Collection

Green Landscape at Cantley, Que., Oil, 45,5 x 56 cm
Private Collection

Trout Fishing at Beauchamp Lake, 1981, Oil, 56 x 71 cm
Masters Gallery, Calgary

Autumn, 1960, Oil, 51 x 66 cm
Private Collection

Old Chelsea, Oil, 56 x 51 cm
Private Collection

Hog's Back, Ottawa, Oil, 51 x 56 cm
Private Collection

Fairy Lake, 1955, Oil, 45,5 x 56 cm
Private Collection

Forest Interior near the Gatineau, 1978, Oil, 40,5 x 51 cm
Collection: Mrs. Louise Marie Laberge

Snow in October, Oil, 101,5 x 127 cm
Private Collection

Trio baroque, 1980
Oil, 45,5 x 61 cm
Collection: Dr. M. Marois

Skaters, Oil, 30,5 x 40,5 cm
L'Art français, Montreal

Guignes Street, Ottawa, 1979, Oil
Collection : Mr. and Mrs. A. Larivière

Jackie, 1970, Sanguine, 35,5 x 43 cm
Private Collection

Nude and Mirror, Watercolour, 35,5 x 40,5 cm
Private Collection

Ennui, Oil, 30,5 x 40,5 cm
L'Art français, Montreal

Studio Corner, Oil, 61 x 76 cm
Private Collection

The Studio in October, 1980, Oil, 71 x 91,5 cm
Kinsman Robinson Galleries, Toronto

Byward Market, Ottawa, 1980, Oil, 45,5 x 61 cm
Private Collection

Fishermen at Cap à l'Aigle, Oil, 40,5 x 51 cm
Private Collection

Gaspe, Les Mechins at Dusk, Oil, 30,5 x 40,5 cm
Collection : Mr. Raphael Shano

Fishermen at Neil's Harbour, N.E., 1967, Watercolour, 34 x 43 cm
Private Collection

Skaters, 1946, Oil, 30,5 x 40,5 cm
Private Collection

Inundation, 1981
Oil, 45,5 x 61 cm
Private Collection

Street in Ottawa, March 1980
Oil, 45,5 x 61 cm
Private Collection

Perkins in Winter
Oil, 96,5 x 114,5 cm
Masters Gallery, Calgary

Spring at Farm Point, Que.
Oil, 96,5 x 114,5 cm
Masters Gallery, Calgary

Skating Rink at St. Sixte, 1980, Oil, 56 x 71 cm
Private Collection

Autumn Snow, Oil, 40,5 x 51 cm
Private Collection

Street in Hull, Oil, 48,5 x 56 cm
Private Collection

March in Hull, Oil, 45,5 x 53,5 cm
Private Collection

Street in Buckingham, Hull, 1980, Oil, 71 x 91,5 cm
Upstairs Gallery, Winnipeg

The Offering, 1969
Oil, 40,5 x 30,5 cm
Collection : Mrs. Jacqueline Brien

Autumn in St. Sixte, 1980, Oil, 96,5 x 114,5 cm
Masters Gallery, Calgary

Fairy Lake
Watercolour, 51 x 35,5 cm
Private Collection

Still Life, Oil, 56 x 71 cm
Private Collection

Flowers in the Studio, Oil, 51 x 61 cm
Private Collection

Quarry in Hull Suburbs, Oil, 45,5 x 53,5 cm
Private Collection

Autumn at Farm Point, Que., Oil, 45,5 x 56 cm
Private Collection

Firewood Delivery, 1946, Oil, 30,5 x 40,5 cm
Private Collection

Children playing in the street, Oil, 51 x 56 cm
Private Collection

Street Musicians, 1981
Oil, 40,5 x 30,5 cm
Private Collection

Contrabassists,
Oil, 30,5 x 25,5 cm
Private Collection

Two Monks, 1950
Oil, 25,5 x 20,5 cm
Collection : The Artist

The Monks, 1953
Casein, 46 x 38 cm
Galerie Vincent, Hull

The Blue Road, Oil, 45,5 x 56 cm
Private Collection

Fairy Lake, 1958, Oil, 51 x 61 cm
Galerie Vincent, Hull

Street in Ottawa, Oil, 38 x 45,5 cm
Private Collection

Scene of Hull, 1945, Oil, 30,5 x 40,5 cm
Private Collection

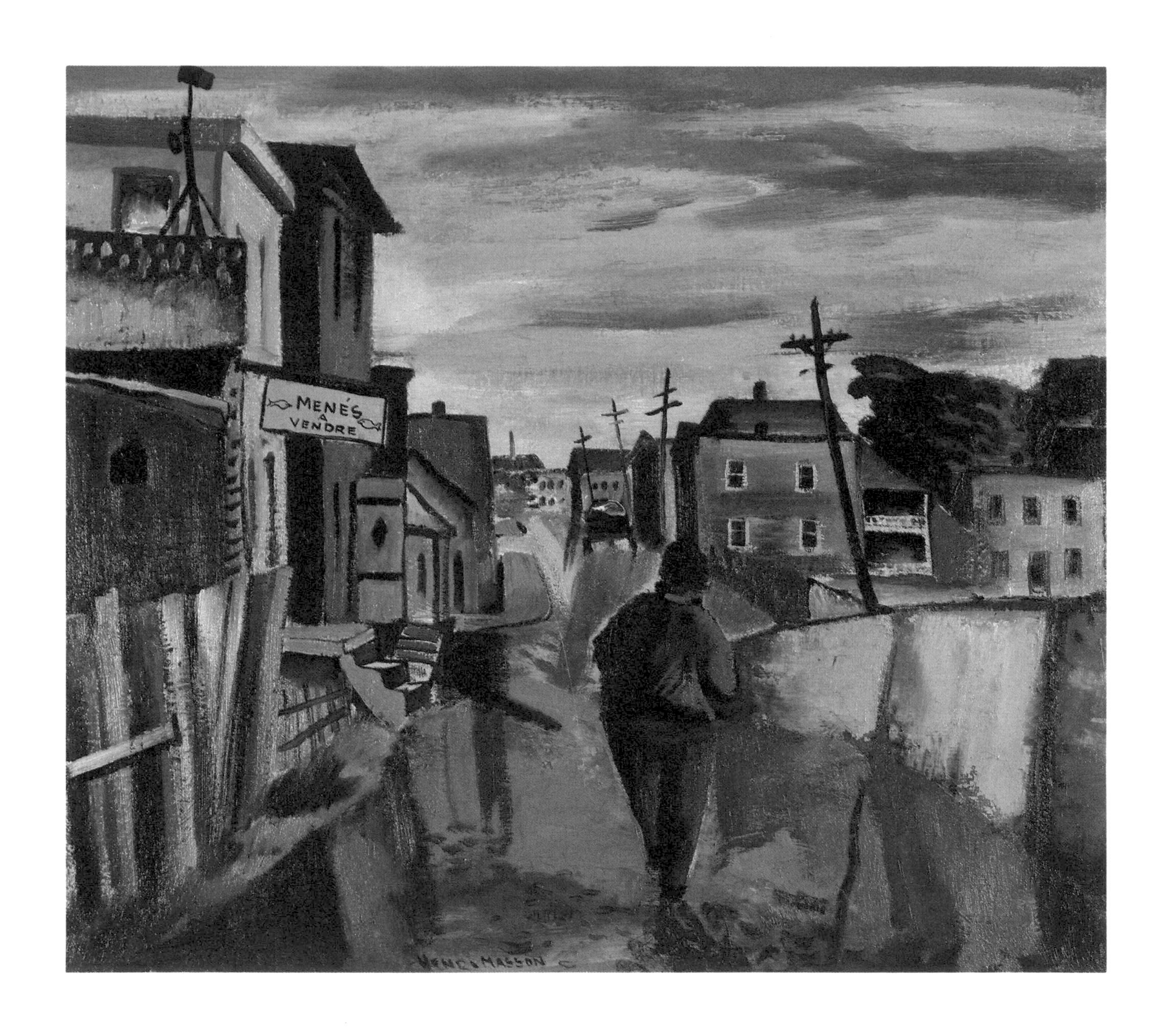

Street in Hull, Oil, 51 x 56 cm
Private Collection

Autumn at Farm Point, Que., Oil, 45,5 x 61 cm
Private Collection

Inundation, Pointe Gatineau, Oil, 44,5 x 53,5 cm
Private Collection

CHRONOLOGY

Henri Masson was born on the 10th of January, 1907, at Spy, near Namur in Belgium, of the marriage of Armand Masson and Berthe Solot.

1919	Death of his father
1921	Arrived in Ottawa, accompanied by his mother.
1923	Entered an engraving atelier in Ottawa. Studied at the Ottawa Art Association and the Ottawa Art Club.
1929	Marriage with Germaine Saint-Denis.
1930	Birth of their daughter, Armande.
1933	First group exhibit, in Ottawa, watercolours, pastels and drawings.
1936	Exhibit of his first oils, at the Ontario Society of Artists, Toronto.
1937	Birth of his first son, Carl. Exhibit at the Caveau.
1938	First solo exhibit, Picture Loan Society, Toronto.
1939	Solo exhibit, the Caveau. Exhibit with the Canadian Group of Painters, Toronto. Exhibit at New York World Fair. Birth of his second son, Jacques. Exhibit at the 57th Spring Salon, Galerie des Arts, Montreal.
1941	Masson enters l'Art français, in Montreal, solo exhibit. Exhibit at the Picture Loan Society, Toronto. Masson elected as a member of the Canadian Group of Painters. Entry into the Canadian Society of Painters in Watercolour, and the Graphic Arts Society.
1942	Solo Exhibit, Contempo Studio, Ottawa. Exhibit at Addison Gallery, Andover, Massachusetts.
1943	Returns to l'Art français. Article on Masson in Geographical Magazine, London.
1944	With H.O. McCurry, A.Y. Jackson and Arthur Lismer, Masson judges a contest for war artists, at the National Gallery. Participates in exhibit at Yale University Art Gallery, New Haven. New exhibit at l'Art français. Solo exhibit, Little Gallery, Ottawa. Exhibit at the Museum of Fine Arts, Rio de Janeiro, Brazil. Documentary by the National Film Board.
1945	Masson leaves the engraving atelier. New exhibit, Little Gallery, Ottawa. Group exhibit, National Gallery. Elected president of the Conference of Canadian Artists, Ottawa. Solo exhibit, Eaton's College Gallery, Toronto.

1946 Exhibit at UNESCO, Paris.

1947 Exhibit at the Little Gallery, Ottawa.

1948 At West Palm Beach, Florida, exhibits with five other Canadian painters at the Norwood Gallery: Roberts, Cosgrove, Milne, Emily Carr, and Fritz Brandtner.
Teaches at Queen's University, Kingston, and at the National Gallery.

1949 Participates, in Boston, in an exhibit mounted by the National Gallery.

1950 Article on Masson, Time magazine, New York.
Exhibit with the Canadian Group of Painters, Toronto Art Gallery.
Exhibit at the London Art Museum, with Harold Town.

1951 Teaches at Queen's University.
Participates in the Biennial, Sao Paulo, Brazil.

1952 First travel in Europe and return to Spy, his birthplace.

1953 Exhibit at the Little Gallery, Ottawa.
Participates in the Colombo Plan Presentation of Modern Art, in New Delhi.
National Gallery, Ottawa, exhibit for the coronation of Queen Elizabeth II.

1954 First exhibit at the Robertson Gallery, Ottawa.
New exhibit at l'Art français.
Teaches for a Summer at Banff School of Fine Arts.
Exhibit at the Foyer de l'Art et du Livre, Ottawa.
Exhibit at Gallery XII, Museum of Fine Arts, Montreal.

1955 Exhibits in Toronto at the Ontario Art Gallery.
Honorary doctorate from Assumption College, Windsor, Ontario.
With A.Y. Jackson, teaches at the Kingsmere Summer Festival.
Exhibit at the Art Museum of Winnipeg.
A Masson painting, «Logs on the Gatineau River», appears as the cover for the Canadian Geographical Journal.

1957 New exhibit at Robertson Gallery.
More travels in Europe (Italy, France, Belgium).

1958 First exhibit at Waddington Gallery, Montreal.

1959 Exhibit at the Laing Gallery, Toronto.

1960 Gives Summer course at the Doon School of Fine Arts. (an experience to be repeated each year until 1963).

1961 New exhibit at l'Art français.

1962 Masson exhibits with the Canadian Group of Painters at Ontario Art Gallery, Toronto.

1963 Exhibit at the National Gallery, with the Canadian Group of Painters.
The Art Museum of London, Ontario.
Canadian masters of painting and sculpture.

1964 First exhibit at Klinkhoff Gallery, Montreal.

1965 Masson illustrates «Quebec in Revolt,» an article on the quiet revolution in Quebec appearing in Fortune magazine.

1967 Exhibit at Art Lenders Gallery, Montreal.

	Exhibit at Wallack Gallery, Ottawa.
1970	Exhibit at the Quebec Pavilion, for the Osaka Exhibit.
1971	Exhibits at Wallack, in Ottawa.
1973	Travels to the Soviet Union.
1974	New exhibition at Klinkhoff. Solo exhibit at the Art Emporium Gallery, Vancouver.
1975	One hour interview broadcast for radio by Radio-Canada.
1975	Editions La Fregate publishes a biography of Henri Masson written by Hughes de Jouvancourt.
1976	New exhibit at Klinkhoff. Second exhibit at the Art Emporium, Vancouver. Travels to the Orient: Japan, Malaysia, Thailand, and Hong Kong.
1978	Masson's works appear in travelling exhibit mounted by the Musée de Québec, and entitled «The Art of Landscape in Quebec, 1800-1940». The exhibit travels throughout the Western and Atlantic Provinces. Exhibits at the Downstairs Gallery, Edmonton.
1979	The municipality of Sainte-Catherine d'Alexandrie, in Quebec, names a street after Masson. Claude Bouchard publishes «Henri Masson — La Vision d'un peintre.» (Popular and deluxe editions). Celebrated Golden Wedding Anniversary.
1980	Appears on television, on the Radio-Canada programme «Rencontres.» In February, a large scale exhibit at Klinkhoff. Masson in a one hour interview with Naïm Kattan, broadcast for the radio séries «L'atelier,» on Radio-Canada's FM band.
1981	In January, a Masson retrospective at the Kinsman-Robertson Gallery, Toronto.

PRINTED BY
PIERRE DESMARAIS INC., MONTREAL

COLOUR SEPARATIONS BY
LITHO ACME, MONTREAL

PHOTOCOMPOSITION BY
ATELIER DE COMPOSITION LHR, CANDIAC